Insights

into

FAITH

Andrew Wommack

Insights into Faith
ISBN: 978-1-881541-18-9

INTRODUCTION

This booklet is based on a COLLECTION of edited footnotes from Andrew Wommack's *Life for Today Study Bible*. Each chapter deals with a different aspect of faith. How does faith operate? What are the three major hindrances to faith? How can I recognize barriers that hinder faith? How can I make the "measure of faith" God has given me more effective? Scripture references are carefully footnoted so you can use your Bible to study along.

The *Life for Today Study Bible* with taped commentarty is available to those who subscribe to the *20/20 Gospel Study Partnership* program by committing to support the outreaches of Andrew Wommack Ministries with a gift of $20.00 or more per month for 20 months. For a complete list of these outreaches and information about this ministry, go to our website at www.awmi.net, call our Helpline at 719-635-1111, or write to:

Andrew Wommack Ministries
P.O. Box 3333
Colorado Springs, CO 80934

CHAPTER 1

Insights Into Faith

Definition of Faith:

FAITH IS YOUR POSITIVE RESPONSE TO WHAT GOD HAS ALREADY DONE. It is your response to God's grace. It is NOT what you must DO to make the Lord act on your behalf. You only need to RESPOND to what He has already done. That is faith.

Faith and Salvation

The new birth (salvation) is essential for entering into the kingdom of God. As Jesus explained to Nicodemus,[1] it is not a

[1]John 3:4

> *We are TOTALLY incapable of saving ourselves, so we need a Savior—Jesus.*

second, physical birth but a spiritual birth. It's regeneration, not are formation. And just as we can't accomplish our physical births, neither can we produce our spiritual rebirths. It is a new creation, which can only be accomplished by a creative miracle of the Holy Spirit.[2] We are TOTALLY incapable of saving ourselves,[3] so we need a Savior—Jesus.[4] We need to BELIEVE in the Lord Jesus Christ in order to be saved.[5] He has already provided salvation for those who BELIEVE, and faith is the only condition.[6]

Faith needs a Savior

Matthew 9:27-31 records a story of two blind men receiving healing from Jesus. Jesus asked them if they believed He was able to heal them. They said, "Yes." Then He said, "Be it done unto you according to your faith." ("According" means "in proportion to.") Jesus did not do their believing for them. The two blind men had sufficient faith to produce their healing, so why hadn't

[2]2 Cor. 5:17; John 1:13, and 3:5
[3]Jer. 13:23; Rom. 3:10-12, 8:7-8;
   and Eph. 2:3
[4]Titus 1:4; 2:13; 3:4, and 6
[5]Acts 16:31
[6]1 Tim. 4:10

they been healed before that day? Because until then, they had no SAVIOR in whom to put their faith. We are to "look unto Jesus," the author and finisher of our faith.[7]

Faith Comes by the Word

Romans 10:17 says, "Faith comes by hearing and hearing by the word." A good example of this truth in action is the story of John the Baptist in prison.[8] Jesus used the Word of God to rouse John's faith—to get him out of doubt and unbelief.

John was alone and despondent, so he sent his disciples to ask Jesus, "Are you the Expected One, or shall we look for someone else?" He was beginning to doubt—even though he had baptized Jesus himself. With his own mouth, he had declared, "Behold, the Lamb of God who takes away the sins of the world!"[9] (It's easy to get into doubt and unbelief when the pressure is on.) Jesus didn't give John a direct answer. Instead, He responded by asking the disciples to report to John all they had "seen and heard." He referred to the prophecies of Isaiah when He told the disciples, "Tell John the blind receive sight and the lame walk. The lepers are cleansed, the deaf hear, the dead are raised up, and the poor have the gospel preached to them."[10] After the disciples walked

[7]Heb. 12:2
[8]Matt. 11:1-19
[9]John 1:29
[10]Is. 29:17-19, 35:3-6, and 61:1-2

> *We need to remember how Jesus responded to John's discourragement—He pointed him back to the WORD.*

away, He then turned to the crowd and heralded John the Baptist as the greatest of all Old Testament prophets.

Why did Jesus do this? Why did He wait until John's disciples were gone to say these great things about him? Wouldn't it have encouraged John to hear that Jesus had announced that he was so great? Why did Jesus not give a direct answer?

Jesus knew that John was very familiar with the prophecies of Isaiah,[11] and He was pointing him back to those scriptures.[12] The faith John needed in order to banish his doubt would come from the Word of God.[13] It may have appeared that Jesus was giving an inadequate reply to John, but He was actually ministering to John in the most powerful way possible. The Word of God is magnified above the name of God and is more trustworthy than the audible voice of God out of heaven.[14]

[11]John 1:22-23
[12]Is. 29:17-19, 35:3-6, and 61:1-2
[13]Rom. 10:17 and Eph. 6:16-17
[14]Ps. 138:2 and 2 Pet. 1:17-20

Sometimes, when we are experiencing periods of doubt and discouragement, we pray for God to do something special to lift us out of our despair. We need to remember how Jesus responded to John's discouragement—He pointed him back to the WORD. We need to go to the Word ourselves and receive the greater blessing of walking by faith and not by sight.[15]

[15]Matt. 8:10 and 2 Cor. 5:7

CHAPTER 2

THE LAW OF FAITH

There MUST be some degree of faith present in the person receiving a miracle or in an intercessor who is praying for miracles. The following stories of healing in the Bible support this fact:

The Woman with the Issue of Blood

Luke 8:43-48 records the story of the woman with the issue of blood. Multitudes were crowding Jesus on all sides, so it seems strange that He would ask "Who touched me?" Many people were physically touching Jesus, but this woman touched His power by faith. Lots of people in the crowd probably needed healing, but this woman is the only person mentioned who received it. The difference was the touch of faith. She believed that she would be healed if she could just touch Him.

If <u>willingness</u> to heal determined whether or not the healing took place, then all of the sick in this multitude would have been healed. This instance illustrates that it is not prayer that saves the sick but rather the "prayer of faith."[1]

Is it possible that Jesus, who was God manifest in the flesh,[2] did not actually know who touched Him? Yes! Although Jesus' spiritual man was divine, He took upon Himself a physical body, which had limitations.[3] Like us, He became tired and hungry.[4] As He grew up, He increased in wisdom and stature.[5] He operated as a sinless man by receiving from His Father through faith.[6] At thirty years of age, Jesus was filled with the Spirit. He was baptized by John and began His public ministry.[7] Miracles began to follow in abundance. He was able to draw on His divine ability through the gifts of the Holy Spirit, just as we can today.[8]

The woman who touched Him was healed BEFORE He discerned what had happened or who had received the power. After Jesus felt the power of God leave Him and heal the woman,

[1]James 5:15
[2]1 Tim. 3:16
[3]Phil. 2:6-8 and Heb. 2:14-18
[4]Luke 4:2 and 8:23
[5]Luke 2:52
[6]John 8:29 and Heb. 11:6

[7]Matt. 3:16
[8]Matt. 4:23-24; Luke 6:8, 19:5;
    John 1:47-48, 4:16-19, 14:12;
    and 1 Cor. 12:7

the woman "saw" that Jesus knew it was her.[9] He had received a word of knowledge from the Holy Spirit.[10] Only then did He single her out.

This illustrates that healing is governed by law, and not by a case-by-case decision from God based on His feelings toward us. This woman received her healing by the law of faith[11] before Jesus knew anything about her. Healing is governed by law! We will not obtain the miracle we seek by impassioned pleas to God to obtain a miracle even though Jesus is touched by our feelings.[12] It requires faith to obtain a miracle.[13] It's not because Jesus doesn't know our needs or hear our cries that miracles don't happen. Many people in the multitude had needs, and they were all thronging Jesus to get those needs met. But miracles don't happen all the time, because very few know how the law of faith works. Even in

We will not obtain the miracle we seek by impassioned pleas to God even though Jesus is touched by our feelings. It requires faith to obtain a miracle.

[9]Luke 8:47
[10]1 Cor. 12:8
[11]Rom. 3:27
[12]Heb. 4:15
[13]Heb. 11:6

Jesus' own hometown, He COULD not (not WOULD not) do many mighty works because of the people's unbelief.[14]

The Widow's Son

The story of the widow's son[15] has mistakenly been used as an example to demonstrate that Jesus produced miracles without any faith from those receiving the miracle—that it was by HIS faith alone.

As Jesus approached the city of Nain, He saw a funeral taking place. A large crowd was following the coffin and grieving mother. His heart went out to the widow, and He told her not to cry. Then He went up to the coffin and said, "Young man, I say to you, get up." The dead man sat up and began to talk.

Whose faith was present in the case of the widow's son? First, the mother of the boy responded to Jesus in faith. She demonstrated a faith response when she allowed Jesus to interrupt the funeral procession and tell her to stop weeping. These people were no different from mourners at funerals today. If this woman had rebelled at Jesus' intrusion, the crowd would have sided with her because of pity. But no reactions of this kind were recorded.

[14]Mark 6:5-6
[15]Luke 7:12-17

She gave all authority to Jesus. In this case, the mother was the intercessor.

Second, it cannot be proven that a dead person has no choice in what happens. From our viewpoint, that may be taken for granted, but the Scriptures do not state that a dead person has a choice whether or not he or she returns to life or remains dead. A person does not cease to exist at death; they simply leave their body. The person is still very much alive. Many people who have been raised from the dead have mentioned that they had a "choice" as to whether or not to reenter their bodies. Although this principle cannot be verified by Scripture, neither can it be ruled out by Scripture.

The Centurion's Great Faith

There are only two times in all of Scripture that say Jesus "marveled." He marveled at the centurion's faith[16] and at the Jew's unbelief.[17] Jesus Himself is the author and finisher of our faith, so faith that could make Jesus marvel is worth examining.

The centurion had a sick servant, so he sent for Jesus. But before Jesus could arrive, the centurion came out and told Jesus

[16]Luke 7:9
[17]Mark 6:6

15

> *The person who simply believes the written Word of God is operating in a much higher form of faith than those who require additional proof.*

not to trouble Himself, but to only say the word and his servant would be healed. He believed that the spoken word of Jesus was sufficient to produce the miracle. He didn't need Jesus to come to his house, because he had faith in Jesus' word. And Jesus marveled at his faith. Therefore, we can see that the person who simply believes the written Word of God is operating in a much higher form of faith than those who require additional proof.[18]

Faith is released by speaking words.[19] God released faith when He SPOKE the creation into being.[20] The faith that made Jesus marvel was faith in the authority of the spoken word. Mark 1:40-45 records an instance of a leper who beseeched Jesus for healing. The leper was healed as soon as Jesus SPOKE. Mark 11:23 says "we shall have whatsoever we SAY if we believe and doubt not in our hearts." We need to pray and believe God's promises for our

[18]John 20:29
[19]Prov. 18:20-21, Rom. 10:8-10, and 2 Cor. 4:13
[20]Gen. 1:3-26

lives, and not be snared by the words of our mouths.[21]

Jesus could have also healed Jairus' daughter by just speaking the Word,[22] but He did as Jairus requested—He went to their house to minister to her (Luke 8:41). This illustrates how the Lord ministers to us according to our faith.[23] Apparently, Jairus' faith would not have received this miracle if Jesus had ministered to him as he did to the centurion. Jairus believed that if Jesus came to his house and prayed, his daughter would be raised up. Therefore, Jesus ministered to him at the level of his faith. (And He didn't rebuke him for having less faith!)[24]

We need to pray and believe God's promises for our lives, and not be snared by the words of our mouths.

Faith Requires Action

Faith can be seen in action. Just as Jesus explained to Nicodemus in John 3:8, faith is like the wind, as it affects life around it. It is invisible, but always accompanied by corresponding

[21]Prov. 6:2
[22]Ps. 107:20
[23]Matt. 9:29
[24]James 1:5

actions, which can be seen (James 2:17-26). Consider the following examples:

The Man with the Palsy

Luke 5:17-25 records the story of a man healed of palsy. Jesus was ministering in a house crowded with people—inside and out. The man with palsy was too weak to even bring himself to the house, so his friends carried him. They lowered him down through the roof to get him to Jesus. Jesus watched their actions and saw their faith.[25] He then rewarded the sick man with forgiveness of sins and healing. (This man had not done any of the "works" that some people teach are required to receive forgiveness of sins, such as water baptism, keeping the Law, etc. His faith in Jesus saved him. Yes, we are to have good works, but holiness is a fruit—not a requirement—of salvation.)

Jesus not only saw the faith of the paralytic, but He saw the faith of his four friends.[26] Jesus saw THEIR faith. This demonstrates that our intercession in faith can powerfully affect others. However, our faith is not a substitute for their faith. Even Jesus could not produce healing in those who would not believe.[27] It is evident that the paralytic had faith, because he was

[25]Luke 5:20
[26]Luke 5:20
[27]Mark 6:5-6

not resistant to the four who brought him. He also got up without help and obeyed Jesus' command.

The Impotent Man at the Pool of Bethesda

In the case of the impotent man at the pool of Bethesda, Jesus asked a question to "spur" him to action.[28] He asked, "Wilt thou be made whole?" On the surface, this might seem like an unnecessary question, but Jesus knew exactly what He was doing. One possible reason might be that the man didn't know who Jesus was, so Jesus approached him with this question to get his attention. Another reason may be that the man had lost the will to fight and Jesus was trying to "provoke" him. His attitude may have been like many people who desire to be healed. They go through the motions of trying to get well, but inwardly, they've lost the will to fight and have fallen into despondency and self pity. One or both of these reasons could have been the motive behind the question.

Our intercession in faith can powerfully affect others. However, our faith is not a substitute for their faith.

[28]John 5:6

19

> *Jesus often told the person to do something to demonstrate faith.*

After the man answered yes, Jesus commanded him to do something that was totally impossible—"Get up, pick up your bed, and walk." Even if the man felt something emotionally or physically, there was still no rational reason why he would be able to do this. To get up and walk would be a total act of faith, and that is precisely why Jesus told the man to do it.

Most of the time, people took a step of faith just by coming to Jesus for healing. But in this instance, Jesus approached him, so the man had made no step of faith. Therefore, it was imperative that Jesus stir up some kind of faith response in him. Because healing does not come without some manifestation of faith on the part of the recipient, Jesus[29] often told people to do something to demonstrate faith.[30]

The Man with the Withered Hand

Matthew 12:9-13 records another example where Jesus required action to express or release faith. This particular man

[29]Mark 6:5-6
[30]Matt. 12:9-14; Luke 7:11-15, 17:12-19; John 9:1-7 and 11:39-44

had a withered hand, and Jesus told him, "Stretch out your hand." The man knew from their conversation that Jesus intended to heal him, and he eagerly complied. It was AFTER he stretched forth his hand that he was healed.

The Blind Beggar in Jerusalem

When Jesus healed the blind beggar in Jerusalem,[31] there was a specific reason why Jesus spat on the ground, made clay, anointed this man's eyes, and then told him to go to the pool of Siloam and wash—faith has to be acted upon.[32]

Jesus didn't heal people without demanding faith from them.

Some have suggested that Jesus did this just to be different. But He did it to give this man a way of acting in faith. This man was unlike most of the people that Jesus healed. Like the man at the pool of Bethesda, he hadn't approached Jesus to ask for healing. If he had, he would have been taking quite a step of faith. (Anyone who openly believed that Jesus was the Christ was automatically excommunicated from the Jewish synagogue.)[33]

[31]John 9
[32]James 2:17-20
[33]John 9:22

> *Any word spoken to us by God carries in itself the anointing and power to fulfill that word—if we will release that power by believing and acting on that word.*

But he had taken no step of faith toward Jesus as the Healer. Instead, he was brought to Jesus' attention by His disciples.

The pool of Siloam was over half a mile away from where Jesus encountered the blind man near the temple grounds. The man could have succumbed to embarrassment, written the whole thing off as foolishness, wiped the clay from his eyes, and resumed begging. The fact that he obeyed Jesus' instructions reveals that there was faith in his heart. Jesus didn't heal people without demanding faith from them. Some degree of faith always has to be present in both the person administering the healing and in the one receiving healing, or in an intercessor who is standing in for them.

Peter Walks On Water

You would think that a great deal of faith would be required to walk on water. Yet, Jesus spoke one word, "Come," and Peter did exactly as he was told.[34] This was spoken by the one who made all things,[35] and it had just as much power in it as the words that were spoken at creation. The power for Peter to walk on the water was in the Word. Likewise, any word spoken to us by God carries in itself the anointing and power to fulfill that word—if we will release that power by believing and acting on that word.

Despite all of the criticism that might be leveled at Peter for becoming afraid and beginning to sink, he did walk on the water. There were eleven other disciples in the boat, and although they clearly saw Jesus and Peter walking on the water, they still did not participate. One of the important steps in receiving a miracle from God is to leave the security of your natural senses (get out of your boat) and put yourself in a position where there has to be a miracle from God to hold you up. God is no respecter of persons.[36] Any of the disciples could have walked on the water if they would have asked—and gotten out of the boat.

[34]Matt. 14:29
[35]John 1:3
[36]Rom. 2:11

CHAPTER 3

HINDRANCE TO FAITH

FEAR: Second Timothy 1:7 says, "God hath not given us the spirit of fear; but of power, and of love, and of a sound mind." First John 4:18 says, "There is no fear in love; but perfect love casteth out fear: because fear hath torment. He that feareth is not made perfect in love."

There are two kinds of fear. The American Heritage Dictionary gives two definitions: "A feeling of alarm or disquiet caused by the expectation of danger, pain, disaster, or the like;

terror; dread; apprehension" and "Extreme reverence or awe, as toward a supreme power."

Godly Fear

Hebrews 12:28 says that there is a godly fear with which we are supposed to serve God. It thereby implies that there is an ungodly fear that is not acceptable in serving God.

Christians are to have reverence, or awe, toward God.[1] God commands us to fear Him. The fear of the Lord is the beginning of knowledge and wisdom.[2] It is also a qualification for leadership.[3] Proverbs 8:13 says that the fear of the Lord is to hate evil. The fear of the Lord is something that can be taught.[4] Also, the phrases "seeking the Lord" and "honoring the Lord" are used interchangeably with "fearing the Lord."[5] The fear of the Lord produces riches, honor, and life.[6] Our lives can be lengthened through fearing the Lord.[7]

In an unbeliever, the fear of the Lord is a great deterrent to sin.[8] However, with those of us who receive the grace of God, it

---

[1]Ps. 89:7, 33:8; Deut. 10:12, 20; Josh. 4:24, 24:14; 1 Sam. 12:14, 24, 25:12, 31:19, 34:7, 9; 2 Cor. 7:1; 2 Kings 17:36; Ps. 2:11, 19:9, 22:23; Eph. 5:21; and Heb. 5:7
[2]Prov. 1:7
[3]Ex. 18:21 and 2 Sam. 23:3
[4]Deut. 4:10 and Ps. 34:11
[5]Ps. 34:9-11
[6]Prov. 22:4
[7]Deut. 6:2
[8]Ex. 20:20; Deut. 5:29, 6:2; and Prov. 16:6

is His GOODNESS that causes us to fear Him and depart from sin.[9]

Ungodly Fear

Those who have been born again should have no dread or terror of God unless they are planning to renounce their faith in Jesus as their Savior.[10] We have a covenant that guarantees acceptance with God as long as we hold fast to our profession of faith in the atoning blood of our Savior, Jesus Christ.[11]

This is not the case with those who do not accept salvation through Jesus. They have every reason to be terrified. There are many examples of where the Bible uses the word "fear" or "terror" in reference to those who reject God.

Satan has always used the ungodly dread or terror to torment godly people.[12]

For those of us who receive the grace of God, it is His GOODNESS that causes us to fear Him and depart from sin.

[9]Josh. 24:2-14; 1 Sam. 12:24; Ps. 130:4, 147:11; Jer. 33:9; Hos. 3:5; and Titus 2:11-12
[10]Heb. 6:6
[11]Eph. 1:5-6; Heb. 4:14, and 10:23
[12]Heb. 2:14-15 and 1 John 4:18

This kind of fear is a real detriment to faith. Faith and fear are OPPOSING forces. Fear is actually faith in reverse. When you are in this kind of fear, you are believing something or someone other than God. Therefore, fear makes us subject to Satan and his death, just as faith makes us recipients of all that God has to offer.[13] This is the reason Jesus told Jairus, "Fear not!" Jairus' fear could have sealed his daughter's death.[14]

It is possible to have both faith and fear working in our hearts at the same time. For that reason, Jesus said, "Believe only."[15] The Scriptures admonish us not to be double minded or to waver. Fear can neutralize faith.[16]

Jairus had a part to play in his miracle. Because God does "exceedingly abundant above all that we ask or think, according to the power that worketh in us,"[17] Jesus needed the positive power of faith working in Jairus, and not the negative force of fear.

Peter's Fear

A good example of fear neutralizing faith is when Peter walked on the water. Peter began to sink because of fear. In Matthew

[13]Heb. 2:15, 2 Tim. 1:7, and John 3:16
[14]Heb. 2:15
[15]Luke 8:50
[16]James 1:5-8 and Matt. 17:20
[17]Eph. 3:20

14:31, Jesus used the word "doubt" in reference to Peter's fear. Fear is simply negative faith or faith in reverse.[18]

Where did this fear come from? Second Timothy 1:7 says, "For God has not given us the spirit of fear; but of power, and of love, and of a sound mind." Fear doesn't come from God. Fear was able to affect Peter because he took his attention off of Jesus and had put it on his situation. Peter also had faith (or he wouldn't have been able to even start walking on the water).

Fear and doubt cannot "just overcome" us; we have to let it in. If Peter had kept his attention on Jesus, he wouldn't have feared. In the same way that faith comes by hearing the Word of God, fear comes by hearing or seeing something contrary to God's Word.[19] We won't be tempted with fear or doubt if we won't consider those things.[20]

> *Fear is simply negative faith or faith in reverse.*

The wind and the waves didn't really have anything to do with Peter walking on the water. He would not have been able to walk on

[18] Luke 8:50
[19] Rom. 10:17
[20] Heb. 11:15

water even if it had been calm. The circumstances simply took Peter's attention away from Jesus and led Him back into carnal thinking.

That's just what Satan tries when he pulls us into thoughts about our problems. But no problem is too big for God. We need to cast our care on God and keep our eyes on Jesus, the living Word.[21]

The entrance of fear and the exit of faith doesn't happen instantly. There are always signs that this is happening. Peter's faith didn't fail him all at once. The Scriptures say he only "began" to sink. If there wasn't any faith present, he would have sank all at once. If we will turn our attention back to Jesus, as Peter did, He will save us from drowning.

The Fear in the Woman with the Issue of Blood

According to the Levitical Law, a person having an issue of blood was unclean. Anyone who touched the unclean person also became unclean.[22] Those who were unclean were responsible for

[21]1 Pet. 5:7 and Heb. 12:2
[22]Lev. 15:19-33

warning others of their uncleanness. They were to avoid public exposure and expect very harsh treatment if detected. This could be one reason the woman with the issue of blood feared and trembled as she confessed that she had touched Jesus and had been healed.[23] And Luke said she confessed this to Jesus "before all of the people."

It is also possible that she had a godly fear, or awe, when she realized the magnitude of what had happened to her. Nearly everyone in Scripture who had the power of God manifested to them reacted in this manner.[24]

Fear of Man

In a discourse to the Jews, Jesus said, "How can ye believe, which receive honour one of another, and seek not the honour that cometh from God only?"[25] In other words, "You cannot believe if you are seeking honor from men instead of seeking honor from God alone."

> *If we will turn our attention back to Jesus as Peter did, He will save us from drowning.*

[23]Luke 8:47
[24]Ex. 3:6, 19:16, 20:18-20;
    Judg. 6:22-23, 13:21-22;
    Ps. 89:7; Dan. 10:7, 11; Matt. 17:6;
    Luke 8:25, 35; Acts 9:6-7; and
    Rev. 1:17

[25]John 5:44

> *You cannot be a "man pleaser" and please God at the same time.*

An integral part of faith is seeking God alone with your whole heart.[26] If you are concerned about what people think in order to gain their approval (or honor), you will never take a stand in faith for anything that might bring criticism. This one thing has stopped many people from receiving from God. You cannot be a "man pleaser" and please God at the same time.[27] Satan uses persecution to steal God's Word and thereby stop our faith.[28] If we want to see faith work, we must say with Paul, "Let God be true, but every man a liar."[29]

Unbelief

When Jesus came down from the Mount of Transfiguration, He was approached by a desperate man with a demon-possessed son. The disciples tried to cure the boy, but were unsuccessful.[30] Jesus did not say that these disciples could not cast out the demon because they didn't have faith; He said it was because they had unbelief.[31] Jesus stated that a very small amount of faith (a mustard

[26]Matt. 6:33 and John 15:7
[27]Heb. 11:6 and Col. 3:22
[28]Matt. 5:10 and Mark 4:4-17
[29]Rom. 3:4
[30]Matt. 17:14-16
[31]Matt. 17:20

seed) is sufficient to remove a mountain if there is no unbelief present to hinder it.

Most people think that you either have faith or you have unbelief—that you can't have both at the same time. However, Jesus told Jairus to "believe only,"[32] implying that faith and fear can operate in us at the same time. This is also the reason James tells us not to be double minded.[33] We CAN have thoughts of faith and thoughts of unbelief at the same time.

The disciples asked, "Why could not we cast him out?" This was a valid question. After all, they had prior successes in casting out devils. If they had not believed that they could cast out devils and if they had not already seen that faith produces deliverances, they wouldn't have been surprised and confused at this result. They did have the faith necessary to cast this devil out, and they knew it. However, they didn't

> *We CAN have thoughts of faith and thoughts of unbelief at the same time.*

[32] Luke 8:50
[33] James 1:5-8

see the same results that they had seen before. That is why they were concerned. So they asked Jesus what the problem was. They wouldn't have asked if they had not believed. They did have faith—the same faith that had effected many other deliverances. The problem wasn't their faith; it was their unbelief.

In this instance, the disciples' unbelief was not a doubt that God's power could produce deliverance, but rather a "natural" unbelief. This type of unbelief comes from a hardened heart—one that is more sensitive to what it sees than what it believes.[34]

Every believer has been given "the measure of faith,"[35] but our unbelief nullifies it. It's like having a team of horses pull a heavy weight. The weight will certainly move, but if there is a team of horses of equal strength pulling from the opposite direction at the same time, the weight won't move. Likewise, unbelief counteracts faith. If we just remove the unbelief, a mustard seed amount of faith will be sufficient to move our problems.

Instead of trying to build huge amounts of faith to overcome our fears and unbelief, we should cut off their source. Then our

[34]Mark 6:52 and 9:20-25
[35]Rom. 12:3

simple "child-like" faith that remains will do the job. It doesn't take BIG faith—just PURE faith.

Those who tolerate high levels of unbelief in their lives will never be able to build their faith big enough to overcome unbelief's negative force. In this condition, the only way for them to receive is to get others to mix their faith with them. They can do that in agreement with others or draw on one of the supernatural ministry gifts in someone else (such as the gift of faith or gift of healing, etc).[36] However, God's best is for us to receive directly from Him. We will only be successful at that when we not only build our faith but also destroy our doubts.

Fasting and prayer will rid you of unbelief. Jesus told the disciples that they would need to pray and fast in order to cast out the demon in the possessed boy. Prayer and fasting do not drive

If we just remove the unbelief, a mustard seed amount of faith will be sufficient to move our problems.

[36] 1 Cor. 12:9

out certain demons; they get rid of unbelief! If the name of Jesus and faith in His name won't do the job, then fasting and prayer won't either. Jesus is saying that fasting and prayer are the way to cast out unbelief.[37]

Unbelief that is a result of ignorance can be overcome by receiving the truth of God's Word.[38] However, the unbelief that hindered the disciples in this case was a "natural" type of unbelief.[39] They had been taught all of their lives to believe what their five senses told them. They were simply dominated by this natural input more than by God's supernatural input (His Word).[40] THE ONLY WAY TO OVERCOME UNBELIEF THAT COMES THROUGH OUR SENSES IS TO DENY OUR SENSES THROUGH PRAYER AND FASTING.[41]

Peter's Unbelief

Just as unbelief hindered the disciples' faith to cast the devil out of the demon-possessed boy, it also caused Peter problems when he walked to Jesus on the water.[42] It was not Jesus' fault that Peter began to sink; it was because Peter doubted.

[37]Matt. 17:21
[38]Rom. 10:17 and 2 Pet. 1:4
[39]Matt. 17:20
[40]Luke 9:1
[41]Matt. 4:2 and 17:21
[42]Matt. 14:28-31

However, Jesus immediately reached out and saved Peter without any hesitation. This shows the willingness and compassion of Jesus to save us regardless of what we've done to bring a problem on ourselves.

What did Peter doubt? He didn't doubt that Jesus could walk on the water; he doubted that he could walk on the water even though Jesus told him he could.

Many people think they are operating in all the faith they need if they are believing that God can perform the miracle that they need. But they aren't using faith that gets results until they believe that God is not only able but willing to give them their answer.

Jesus is saying that fasting and prayer are the way to cast out unbelief.

Many people who believe God heals have not been healed. They haven't believed that God has given them the power to receive that

healing. Just as in Peter's situation, Satan doesn't cast doubt on God's ability to perform but on our ability to receive.

Unbelief of Others

The unbelief of others can hinder the manifestation of God's power.[43] For this reason, "Jesus could do no mighty work" in His hometown. He put out all of the mourners who mocked Him in the story of Jairus,[44] and He led the blind man away from the unbelief of others in the town of Bethsaida.[45] He also took a deaf and dumb man aside from the multitude.[46] And Elijah, Elisha, and Peter sought seclusion when raising people from the dead.[47]

Many miracles have been lost, not because of any unwillingness on God's part, but rather because the person who was believing for the miracle failed to realize the hindrance of other people's unbelief. The story of the blind man of Bethsaida is an example of other people's unbelief hindering the manifestation of faith.[48] John 5:19 says Jesus did nothing of Himself but only what He saw His Father do. There was a purpose for leading this man out of the town. Bethsaida was one of the cities that received Jesus' harshest rebuke because of the people's hardened hearts of

---

[43]Mark 6:5-6
[44]Luke 8:51 and Prov. 22:10
[45]Mark 8:22-23
[46]Mark 7:32-33
[47]1 Kings 17:19, 2 Kings 4:32-33, and Acts 9:40

[48]Mark 8:22-23

unbelief.[49] Therefore, it is probable that Jesus led this man away from the crowd to separate him from the unbelief of others.

It is a mistake to assume that God's will automatically comes to pass. It is God's will that no one should perish, but many do perish, and it is because of their unbelief.[50] It is God's will that we all be healed,[51] but not all are healed, because we fail to believe.[52] We play a part in receiving from God. If Jesus, who had no limitations, couldn't do all the mighty works that He desired to do, because of other people's unbelief,[53] then that can certainly happen to us. We have to take into account the level of people's faith. This is the reason Jesus sought seclusion when performing certain miracles.[54]

Jesus did something else unusual with the blind man of Bethsaida. After He prayed for the blind man, He inquired about the results.[55] It was unusual for Jesus to do this, but it was even more unusual that Jesus laid hands on this man a second time. Although others prayed more than once to obtain results in the Old Testament,[56] this is the only example in the New Testament where Jesus ministered to any need more than once to effect a total healing. Because Bethsaida's people had such hardened

[49]Matt. 11:20-22 and Luke 10:13-14
[50]John 3:16
[51]Matt. 8:16-17
[52]Heb. 4:2
[53]Mark 6:5-6
[54]Luke 8:51

[55]Mark 8:22-26
[56]1 Kings 17:21-22, 18:42-45; and
    2 Kings 4:32-35

> *It is a mistake to assume that God's will automatically comes to pass.*

hearts of unbelief, Jesus felt a need to separate this man and pray again.

Jesus didn't request a miracle from God and then look at the circumstances to see if God answered His prayer. That would be walking by sight and not by faith.[57] This is not how Jesus taught us to pray and receive.[58] He also didn't lay hands on this man a second time because He thought His Father didn't hear Him the first time. The man received partial sight the first time Jesus prayed, so it is evident that God's healing power was at work. Jesus also didn't pray a second time because He wasn't sure what the will of the Father was in this case.[59] He really wasn't "asking" a second time—He wasn't doubting God. He knew that manifestations of God's power could be hindered by the unbelief of others, so He continued the ministry elsewhere. He simply gave another "dose" of the anointing power of God. Satan may hinder, but he cannot overcome someone who continues resisting him.

[57] 2 Cor. 5:7
[58] Mark 11:22-24
[59] John 5:19

40

We only need to petition God once for a need. Then we need to believe that we receive.[60] If we petition God more than once, we did not really believe that we received the first time. However, we need and should continue to pray until we receive our manifestation, just as Jesus did with this blind man.

> *We only need to petition God once for a need.*

Are we to "ignore" all evidence contrary to our prayer? Many people, in an effort to walk by faith, pray for God's power to manifest in a situation and then ignore all evidence to the contrary. That does show more faith than responding to circumstances in unbelief, but it falls short of Jesus' example. The best thing to do is exactly what Jesus did. Believe that you receive when you pray to such a degree that you can confront anything to the contrary and overcome it by continuing to apply the power of God. Perseverance in prayer will overcome Satan, not denial. "The effectual prayer of a righteous man availeth much."[61] James 4:7 says we are to submit ourselves to God and resist the enemy.

[60]Mark 11:24
[61]James 5:16

A Hardened Heart

> *Our hearts will become hardened when we meditate or ponder ANYTHING other than God and His ways.*

Our hearts can become hardened by obvious sin such as bitterness, rebellion, anger, disobedience, adultery, murder, self-centeredness, and un-forgiveness. In Mark 11:24-25, Jesus said, "What things soever ye desire, when ye pray, believe that ye receive them, and ye shall have them. And when ye stand praying, forgive." Forgiveness is essential to getting your prayers answered. In Luke 17:5, the disciples asked Jesus, "Increase our faith." It is interesting to note that the apostles asked Jesus to increase their faith after He taught about FORGIVENESS—not miracles. Even after observing all of the wonderful miracles of Jesus, they had never asked for greater faith. It takes faith to walk in love and forgiveness.

A person in total rebellion to God will certainly have a hard heart, but you don't HAVE to be in rebellion to be hardened. In Mark 6:48-52, the disciples were laboring at the oars of a boat in a storm when Jesus came alongside walking on the water. The Word says that they had hardened hearts because they were "sore amazed in themselves beyond measure, and wondered" when they saw Him coming toward them. In this instance, the word "hardened" means "to make calloused, unyielding, cold in spirit, or insensitive to." If we use this Bible definition of a hardened heart, then all of us have areas in our lives where we are insensitive (hardened) to God. The disciples were not in rebellion. They weren't thinking sinful things. Their minds were totally occupied with the storm and how they were going to survive. They were so sensitive to the natural world and its limitations that they were overwhelmed to see Jesus supercede these laws by walking on water.

Our hearts will become hardened when we meditate or ponder ANYTHING other than God and His ways. Even though they had just witnessed the miracle of the fish and loaves, they were in fear and unbelief as they looked at the wind and the waves. And Jesus Himself had commanded them out on the sea. Certainly He wouldn't forsake them! Their minds should have been filled with thoughts of a miraculous rescue.

> *We must remain sensitive to God to keep our hearts from becoming hardened to Him.*

If they had kept their minds on that miracle, they wouldn't have been so amazed when Jesus came walking on the water. Mark 6:48 says Jesus had been watching them from the shore during the storm and had seen them straining at the oars. They could see Him, too, so they had to know that He was aware of their situation. They should have expected Him to do something—even if He had to walk on water to do it. But their fear canceled out their faith. When Jesus caught up to them, His first words were, "Take courage. Don't be afraid." Their hardened hearts kept them from perceiving the spiritual truths of the miraculous power of God, so they were dominated by natural thinking, which is completely inadequate to solve a problem.

The whole universe is founded upon the laws of God, and His revelation truths are "hidden" for His children. When we receive the spiritual rebirth, we are entitled to the revelation of the mysteries of the kingdom.[62] The deep things of God are reserved for us. The "natural" man cannot receive the things of

[62]John 7:17, 14:26, 15:15, 26;
 1 Cor. 2:10, and 16

44

the Spirit, because they are spiritually discerned.[63] Therefore, any person who rejects Jesus as their Savior also rejects the source of all wisdom and knowledge.[64] Their rejection of wisdom also safeguards the laws of God from being appropriated and misused by Satan's kingdom.

God reveals His truths to us in stages.[65] As we walk in the revelations that God has already shown us, He will reveal more to us, and we will have that abundant life that Jesus provided for us on the cross.[66] But those who do not receive God's revelation will lose whatever truth they had, and they will go further and further into deception. Their hearts become hardened.[67]

Hardness of heart is not something we are born with, and it doesn't suddenly strike out of nowhere. In Matthew 13:15, it says "the people's hearts waxed gross." The term "waxed" means "to become gradually more intense or to increase." It is something that is nurtured over a long period of time. This is why we shouldn't violate our consciences—even in the small things. We must remain sensitive to God to keep our hearts from becoming hardened to Him. If we will stay faithful to God in the

[63]1 Cor. 2:14
[64]Col. 2:2-3
[65]Is. 28:9-10
[66]John 10:10 and 2 Pet. 1:3
[67]Mark 6:52

small things, then we'll be strong to remain faithful in the bigger things.[68]

Characteristics of a Hardened Heart

Hardened hearts keep us thinking only in the natural realm.

In Mark 8:17, Jesus explains that a hardened heart blinds us to spiritual perception.[69] It keeps us from understanding spiritual truths. If a person doesn't understand God's Word, then Satan will find no resistance when he comes to steal the Word away.[70] (This is why everyone in the same church service can hear exactly the same message and some will not receive it.) The Word is not the variable—the condition of the heart is.[71]

Hardened hearts keep us thinking only in the natural realm. This is what Jesus is referring to in Matthew 16:8 when He talks to the disciples about their "small faith." They could not perceive the spiritual meaning of the word "leaven." But the words that Jesus spoke were spirit and life,[72] so He was not speaking of yeast—He was speaking of the hypocritical doctrine of the Pharisees.[73]

[68]Luke 16:10-12,
    10:13-27, 11:10, and 14:3-4
[69]Luke 8:12
[70]Ex. 7:10-13, 22; 8:8-15, 19,
    31-32; 9:5-7; 10-12, and 22-34

[71]Luke 8:11 and 15
[72]John 6:63
[73]Luke 12:1

By comparing these two verses, it can be seen that "small faith" and a "hardened heart" are the same. Hebrews 3:12-13 also relates an "evil heart of unbelief" to a hardened heart.

Although a hard heart can keep us from remembering spiritual lessons, it doesn't keep us from recalling facts or scriptures. The disciples in Mark 8:19-21 remembered the facts of the two miraculous feedings, but they forgot the spiritual lessons they had learned. (Some people can quote Scripture and remember a sermon, but they can't remember the spiritual application.) In Job 39:13-17, God speaks of the ostrich who was hardened toward her young. He says that she has no wisdom or common sense. It's like having spiritual retardation. This is why people can know what the Word says and still not see it work. They are more sensitive to fear and doubt than they are to the truths of God's Word. This is what happens when we spend time thinking about things that minister fear and doubt. (As the computer world says, "Garbage in—garbage out.")

CHAPTER 4

INCREASING IN FAITH

We would all like to increase our faith. We want to see miracles! What do the Scriptures have to say about the various degrees of faith?[1]

The Believer's Faith

At salvation, every believer is given the supernatural faith of God. We had to use that faith (not human faith) to believe the Gospel. It came to us through hearing the Word of God.[2] Once we are born again, it becomes an abiding fruit of the Spirit within us.[3]

[1]Matt. 6:30, 8:10, 26, 14:31,
   16:8; and 2 Cor. 10:15
[2]Eph. 2:8 and Rom. 10:17
[3]Gal. 5:22-23

We do have enough faith—we just have to use it without the hindrance of unbelief.

We are all given the same measure of faith at salvation,[4] but not all believers use what God has given them. The Scriptures talk of growing in faith, having little faith, and having great faith, but it is important to understand that they are referring to how much faith we USE—not how much faith we were given. Romans 12:3 says all believers were given "the" same measure of faith.

Jesus' example of the grain of mustard seed underscores the truth that our faith is sufficient.[5] With mustard-seed faith, we can say to a tree, "Be thou plucked up by the root, and be thou planted in the sea." So, we do have enough faith—we just have to use it without the hindrance of unbelief.

We can reverse the unbelief in our lives by using the same laws that harden hearts in a positive way. If faith comes from "hearing and hearing by the word,"[6] then we can actually harden our hearts to doubt and unbelief by considering ONLY God's

[4]Rom. 12:3, 2 Pet. 1:1, and Gal. 2:20
[5]Luke 17:6
[6]Rom. 10:17

Word. A possible and obtainable goal is to become just as sensitive to God and faith as we have been to Satan and doubt. Our faith can grow.[7]

There is more to prayer than simply asking God for things and believing the promises. We must also continue to resist the devil's hindrances by praying the prayer of agreement,[8] the prayer of praise,[9] the prayer of intercession, the prayer of binding and loosing,[10] and the laying on of hands.[11]

The purpose of faith is to serve God—not ourselves. Every area that we use our faith should bring glory to God. We must get out of a self-serving attitude when it comes to our faith.[12] (We are to walk in faith AND love.)[13]

When the disciples asked Jesus to increase their faith,[14] He used the parable of the servant to illustrate this point. If we will be more concerned about using our faith to serve our MASTER instead of serving ourselves, we won't find

> *The purpose of faith is to serve God—not ourselves.*

[7]2 Cor. 10:15
[8]Matt. 18:19
[9]Ps. 8:2 and Matt. 21:16
[10]Matt. 18:18
[11]Mark 16:18
[12]James 4:3

[13]Rom. 12:10 and Eph. 5:2
[14]Luke 17:7-10

ourselves worrying about our own needs. ("Seek ye first the kingdom of God, and his righteousness; and all these things shall be added unto you.")[15] The Lord expects all of His children to live a supernatural life of faith. Living by faith is not only for "super saints"; it's for every born-again believer.

[15]Matt. 6:33

About the Author

For over four decades Andrew Wommack has traveled America and the world teaching the truth of the Gospel. His profound revelation of the Word of God is taught with clarity and simplicity, emphasizing God's unconditional love and the balance between grace and faith. He reaches millions of people through the daily *Gospel Truth* radio and television programs, broadcast both domestically and internationally. He founded Charis Bible College in 1994 and has since established a CBC extension schools in Chicago, Atlanta, Dallas, Jacksonville, Kansas City, and abroad in England and Russia. Andrew has produced a library of teaching materials available in print, audio, and visual formats. And, as it has been from the beginning, his ministry continues to distribute free audio materials to those who cannot afford them.

Other Teachings
by Andrew Wommack

Spirit, Soul & Body

Understanding the relationship of your spirit, soul, and body is foundational to your Christian life. You will never truly know how much God loves you or believe what His Word says about you until you do. In this teaching, learn how they're related and how that knowledge will release the life of your spirit into your body and soul. It may even explain why many things are not working the way you had hoped.

Item Code: 318   Paperback
Item Code: 418   Study Guide
Item Code: 701   Paperback in Spanish
Item Code: 1027-C 4-CD audio album
Item Code: 1027-D As Seen on TV DVD album

The True Nature of God

Are you confused about the nature of God? Is He the God of judgment found in the Old Testament or the God of mercy and grace found in the New Testament? Andrew's revelation on this subject will set you free and give you a confidence in your relationship with God like never before. This is truly nearly-too-good-to-be-true news!

Item Code: 308   Paperback
Item Code: 1002-C 5-CD album

You've Already Got It!

Are you trying to get the Lord to heal, bless, deliver, or prosper you? If so, stop it! God has already done all He will ever do for you. How can that be? As you discover the balance between grace and faith, you'll understand that you've already got everything you need. Never again will you beg God for anything. You'll just believe, release, and receive!

Item Code: 320	Paperback
Item Code: 420	Study Guide
Item Code: 1033-C	6-CD album
Item Code: 1033-D	DVD album

A Better Way to Pray

Prayer is something that every Christian knows they need to do, but very few Christians feel they're successful. There are many reasons, but surprisingly, the biggest is rooted in all the wrong teaching they've received. In this teaching, Andrew counters many widely accepted religious traditions and establishes a foundation upon which a rewarding and effective prayer life can be built.

Item Code: 321	Paperback
Item Code: 1042-C	5-CD album
Item Code: 1042-D	DVD album

Effects of Praise

Every Christian wants a stronger walk with the Lord. But how do you get there? Many don't know the true power of praise. It's essential! These biblical truths will not only spark your understanding but will help promote spiritual growth so you can experience victory.

Item Code: 309   Paperback
Item Code: 1004-C   3-CD album

Thoughts

Thoughts

Thoughts